Halloween Makeup

Safety Guidelines

Patch Test:

Test makeup on a small area of skin 24 hours before full application to check for allergies.

Use Safe Products:

Only use high-quality, non-toxic face paints and cosmetics designed for skin. Avoid using craft paints or markers.

Eye and Lip Safety:

Be cautious near the eyes and mouth. Use products labeled safe for these sensitive areas, and avoid non-cosmetic glitter around the eyes.

Maintain Hygiene:

Wash hands before applying makeup and use clean tools. Avoid sharing makeup to prevent the spread of bacteria.

Proper Ventilation:

Use aerosol sprays and adhesives in a well-ventilated area to avoid inhaling fumes.

Limit Wear Time:

Avoid wearing makeup for extended periods. If possible, remove it after a few hours to prevent irritation.

Safe Removal:

Use a gentle makeup remover or cleanser, and follow with moisturizer. Avoid scrubbing your skin harshly.

Allergy Awareness:

Check labels for potential allergens. If irritation occurs, remove makeup immediately and wash the affected area with mild soap and water.

Contact Lens Caution:

Use only FDA-approved cosmetic lenses and follow the instructions carefully to avoid eye irritation or infection.

General Instructions

Start with a Clean Face:

Ensure your face is clean and dry before applying makeup. This helps the makeup adhere better and last longer.

Layer and Blend:

Apply lighter colors first, gradually adding darker shades. Blend well for a smooth transition between hues.

Set Your Makeup:

Use a setting powder or spray to prevent smudging and keep makeup in place throughout the event.

Coordinate with Costume:

Match your makeup with your costume to create a cohesive and polished look.

Take Your Time:

Allow plenty of time for application to avoid mistakes and enjoy the creative process.

Plan for Touch-Ups:

Bring along a small makeup kit for touch-ups, especially if you'll be wearing your makeup for an extended period.

By following these guidelines, you can ensure a stunning Halloween look while keeping your skin safe and healthy. Enjoy your transformation and have a fantastic Halloween!

Zombie Horror

What You Need:

Green face paint or light green foundation – to create a dead, decaying skin tone.

Black and purple eyeshadow – to accentuate sunken eyes.

Black face paint or eyeliner – for drawing scars and enhancing facial contours.

Fake blood – to create realistic wounds.

Cosmetic latex – to model raised scars and wounds.

Yellow tooth paint – to give teeth a rotten appearance.

Makeup brushes – various sizes for applying the base, blending eyeshadow, and adding details.

Makeup sponge – for applying foundation and paints.

Setting spray – to ensure the makeup stays intact and fresh throughout the night.

How to Create the Look:

Base: Start by applying green face paint or light green foundation evenly across the entire face. This will create a smooth, decayed base that reflects the rotting effect of a zombie. Ensure the paint is well blended, covering all areas of the face.

Eyes: Apply black eyeshadow to the eyelids, blending it towards the crease to add depth and a dark, eerie appearance to the eyes. Then, apply purple eyeshadow around the eyes to achieve a sunken eye effect. Use black face paint or eyeliner to draw dark lines and shadows under the eyes, creating a tired and terrifying look.

Wounds: Use cosmetic latex to create raised scars and wounds on the forehead, cheeks, and chin. Apply latex to selected areas, shaping it into wounds. Then, add fake blood around the scars to give them a realistic, fresh look. You can also add drops of blood on the cheeks or the corners of the mouth for a more infected appearance.

Mouth and Teeth: Apply yellow tooth paint to your teeth to create a rotten effect. Cover your lips with a thin layer of black face paint to emphasize their dead appearance. You can also add some fake blood at the corners of the mouth to make them look infected.

Final Touches and Setting: Finally, set the entire look using a setting spray to ensure that the makeup stays in place all night. Make sure all the details are perfected and that the paint and fake blood look realistic.

Vampiric Nightmare

What You Need:

White face paint or very light foundation – to create a pale, ghostly base.

Black eyeshadow – for creating deep, hollow eyes.

Red face paint or liquid lipstick – for adding bloody accents and dramatic details.

Black eyeliner or face paint – for outlining and creating sharp, sinister details around the eyes and mouth.

Brown or dark red lip color – to define the lips with a vampiric touch.

Makeup brushes – various sizes for applying the base, blending eyeshadow, and detailing.

Setting spray – to ensure the makeup stays in place and vibrant throughout the night.

How to Create the Look:

Base: Begin by applying white face paint or a very light foundation evenly over the entire face. This will create a smooth, pale base that gives a ghostly, undead appearance. Make sure to blend it well into the hairline and down the neck for a seamless look.

Eyes: Apply black eyeshadow around the entire eye area, extending it outward and upward to create a dramatic, hollowed-out effect. Use black eyeliner or face paint to draw sharp, winged shapes around the eyes, extending them toward the temples. Add red face paint or liquid lipstick along the edges of the black areas, blending it slightly into the black to create a bloodshot, sinister effect.

Details: Use black eyeliner or face paint to draw fine lines extending from the eyes, creating the appearance of cracked skin or veins. You can also add some red accents to enhance the effect, making the eyes look more intense and terrifying.

Mouth: Apply a brown or dark red lip color to the lips, defining them with a sharp, vampiric look. Outline the lips with black eyeliner or face paint to add contrast and depth, and blend the color slightly for a smudged, eerie effect.

Final Touches and Setting: Once you are satisfied with the look, set the makeup with a setting spray to ensure it stays intact throughout the night. This step is crucial, especially for a look as detailed and intense as this one.

Carnival Clown Nightmare

What You Need:

White face paint or very light foundation – to create a ghostly, clown-like base.

Purple and black eyeshadow – for dramatic eye accents.

Black and pink face paint or eyeliner – for outlining and creating graphic clown details.

Green hair spray or wig – to achieve the wild, eerie hairstyle.

Makeup brushes – various sizes for applying the base, blending eyeshadow, and adding precise details.

Setting spray – to ensure the makeup stays vibrant and intact.

How to Create the Look:

Base: Start by applying white face paint or very light foundation evenly across the entire face. This will create a smooth, ghostly base reminiscent of a traditional clown, but with a creepy twist. Make sure to cover all areas, including the neck, for a seamless look.

Eyes: Use purple eyeshadow around the eyes, extending it outward to create exaggerated, bold shapes typical of clown makeup. Apply black eyeshadow around the purple areas to add depth and create a more sinister look. Blend the colors to avoid harsh lines, but keep the overall shape sharp and defined.

Clown Details: With black face paint or eyeliner, outline the eye shapes, and add triangle designs above and below the eyes. Use pink face paint to add accents to the triangles, blending slightly into the purple for a gradient effect. Draw exaggerated smile lines from the corners of the mouth, extending them outward and upward, and add stitch-like lines across them for a creepy, stitched-mouth effect.

Hair: Style your hair with green hair spray or wear a green wig to replicate the wild, chaotic look. Ensure the hair is tousled and spiked for maximum effect.

Final Touches and Setting: Complete the look by setting the makeup with a setting spray to keep everything in place throughout the event. Double-check all details to make sure they're sharp and well-defined.

Inferno Demon

What You Need:

White face paint or very light foundation – to create a stark, contrast-rich base.

Red and black face paint – for creating the fiery demonic details.

Black eyeliner or face paint – to outline and add depth to the designs.

Makeup brushes – various sizes for applying the base, blending colors, and detailing.

Small devil horns – for attaching to the forehead to complete the demonic look.

Flame effect wig or props – to simulate flames around the head.

Setting spray – to lock in the makeup and ensure it lasts throughout the night.

How to Create the Look:

Base: Start by applying white face paint or a very light foundation evenly over the entire face and neck. This will create a clean, smooth base that allows the fiery and demonic colors to pop against the skin.

Demonic Details: Begin by outlining the design with black face paint or eyeliner, creating sharp, flame-like shapes across the forehead, around the eyes, and extending down the cheeks. Fill in the areas between these lines with a deep red face paint, blending it slightly with the black to create a fiery gradient effect.

Eyes: Use black face paint to create hollow, deep eye sockets, extending the paint around the eyes and blending it outward for a dramatic, sunken look. Add red accents around the edges to enhance the fiery theme.

Mouth and Nose: Paint the nose in black, shaping it into a skeletal form to enhance the demonic appearance. For the mouth, use black face paint to draw sharp, jagged teeth extending from the lips to the cheeks, simulating a monstrous, skeletal grin. Outline the teeth with red to add depth and contrast.

Horns and Flames: Attach small devil horns to your forehead using skin-safe adhesive. For an added effect, use a flame-themed wig or attach flame props around the head to create the illusion of being engulfed in fire.

Final Touches and Setting: Once all the details are complete, set the makeup with a setting spray to ensure it stays vibrant and in place throughout your event. Double-check the blending and make sure the horns and flame effects are securely attached.

Sinister Circus Clown

What You Need:

White face paint – to create the classic clown base.

Red and black face paint or eyeliner – for creating sharp, menacing clown features.

Blue eyeshadow – for adding bold, dramatic eye accents.

Red lipstick – to enhance the sinister smile.

Clown nose – a bright red, exaggerated nose for the classic clown look.

Makeup brushes – various sizes for applying the base, blending, and detailing.

Clown wig or colored hair spray – to match the wild clown aesthetic.

Setting spray – to keep the makeup in place throughout the event.

How to Create the Look:

Base: Start by applying a layer of white face paint evenly across the entire face. This will serve as the base for your sinister clown look. Make sure the paint is smooth and evenly applied, covering every inch of the face and neck.

Eyes: Apply blue eyeshadow above the eyes, extending it outward to create bold, exaggerated shapes. Use black face paint or eyeliner to outline the blue areas and add depth around the eyes, making them appear more dramatic and intense. Add sharp, red lines extending from the corners of the eyes, curving them upwards and downwards to create a menacing, jagged effect.

Clown Features: Use red face paint to draw the iconic clown smile, extending it well beyond the natural lip line and curving it upward toward the cheeks. Add black detailing around the mouth and eyes to give the smile a sinister twist, making it look more like a sneer. Don't forget to add the exaggerated red nose—this is essential for the classic clown appearance.

Mouth: Fill the lips with red lipstick, matching the intensity of the clown smile. You can add black detailing to the corners of the mouth to make the smile appear more evil and twisted.

Hair: Use a clown wig or apply colored hair spray to achieve the wild, unruly hair typical of a sinister clown. Go for bright colors like red or orange to match the overall aesthetic.

Final Touches and Setting: Once the look is complete, set the makeup with a setting spray to ensure it stays in place throughout your event. Make sure all details are sharp, and the colors are vibrant.

Chaotic Clown

What You Need:

White face paint or very light foundation – to create the signature pale clown base.

Black and purple eyeshadow – for creating deep, dramatic eyes.

Red face paint or lipstick – to craft the iconic, smeared smile.

Black eyeliner – for adding sharp details around the eyes.

Green hair spray or temporary dye – to achieve the disheveled green hair look.

Makeup brushes and sponges – various sizes for applying and blending makeup.

Setting spray – to keep the makeup intact throughout your event.

How to Create the Look:

Base: Start by applying a layer of white face paint or very light foundation evenly across the entire face. This will serve as the base, giving you the pale, clown-like complexion. Blend well into the hairline and down the neck to create a seamless finish.

Eyes: Use black eyeshadow to create dark, hollowed-out areas around the eyes, blending it outward for a dramatic effect. Then, add purple eyeshadow around the black areas to create a bruised, chaotic appearance. With black eyeliner, draw sharp lines extending from the outer and inner corners of the eyes, enhancing the menacing look.

Clown Smile: Using red face paint or lipstick, draw an exaggerated, smeared smile that extends from the lips towards the cheeks. Make sure the lines are uneven and slightly messy to give the look a chaotic, disturbed vibe. You can use your fingers or a brush to smudge the edges for a more realistic effect.

Details: Add small, sharp lines around the eyes with black eyeliner to simulate wrinkles and enhance the aged, worn-out appearance. You can also add some red accents around the eyes and cheeks to intensify the chaotic look.

Hair: Use green hair spray or temporary dye to color your hair, then style it into a messy, disheveled look. The more chaotic, the better – this character thrives on disorder.

Final Touches and Setting: After you've completed the makeup, set it with a setting spray to ensure it stays in place all night. Make sure the colors are vivid and the details are sharp to maintain the intense, unsettling effect.

Shadow Demon

What You Need:

White face paint or very light foundation – to create a pale, ghostly base.

Black face paint or eyeshadow – for creating deep, shadowy accents.

Black eyeliner – to outline and enhance the demonic details.

Red contact lenses – to give the eyes a haunting, otherworldly appearance.

Small black horns – to complete the demon look.

Makeup brushes – various sizes for applying and blending the makeup.

Setting spray – to ensure the makeup stays intact throughout the night.

How to Create the Look:

Base: Start by applying a layer of white face paint or very light foundation evenly across the entire face. This will create a stark, ghostly base that will make the dark accents pop. Be sure to blend it well into the hairline and down the neck for a cohesive look.

Eyes: Use black face paint or eyeshadow to create deep, hollowed-out areas around the eyes, blending it outward to create a shadowy, smoky effect. Extend the black up towards the forehead and outwards, forming sharp, flame-like shapes for a demonic, fiery look. Use black eyeliner to define the edges and add more detail, making the eyes appear more menacing.

Details: With black eyeliner or face paint, draw sharp, intricate designs extending from the eyes towards the temples and cheeks, mimicking dark, demonic flames or cracks in the skin. Outline the lips with black, drawing jagged, teeth-like lines extending from the corners of the mouth to give a skeletal, grimacing effect.

Horns: Attach small black horns to the forehead using skin-safe adhesive. Position them symmetrically for a balanced, demonic appearance. The horns add an essential element to the look, making it unmistakably otherworldly.

Final Touches: Insert red contact lenses to give your eyes a terrifying, otherworldly glow, amplifying the demonic presence of the character. Once all the makeup is applied and the horns are in place, set the look with a setting spray to ensure it lasts through the entire event

Cursed Pirate

What You Need:

Green and black face paint – for creating the cursed, undead look.

Black eyeliner – to outline and define the eyes and facial details.

Red face paint – for adding small, eerie details like blood or markings.

Skull and crossbones temporary tattoo or sticker – to enhance the pirate theme.

Makeup brushes – various sizes for applying and blending the paint.

Pirate accessories – such as a bandana, hoop earring, and facial hair (drawn or real) to complete the pirate aesthetic.

Setting spray – to ensure the makeup lasts throughout your event.

How to Create the Look:

Base: Start by applying green face paint to one side of the forehead, blending it into the skin to create a decayed, cursed effect. Use a sponge or brush to diffuse the edges, making the green look like it's seeping through the skin. Leave the other side of the face in its natural tone to maintain the dual nature of the "cursed" and "human" pirate.

Eyes: Apply black face paint or eyeshadow around the eyes, extending it outward to create a sunken, hollow effect. Use black eyeliner to draw sharp, jagged lines around the eyes, giving them a dramatic and menacing look. Add a touch of red face paint for small blood-like details around the eyes to intensify the cursed, undead vibe.

Facial Details: Use black eyeliner to draw and enhance the facial hair, creating sharp, stylized beard lines that mimic a classic pirate look. Add intricate details like thin scars or cracks along the skin with black face paint, emphasizing the cursed, battle-worn appearance.

Pirate Markings: Apply a skull and crossbones temporary tattoo or sticker to the forehead, directly above the eyebrows, to signify the pirate's allegiance to the dark and cursed sea.

Final Touches: Accessorize with a red bandana tied around the head, and add a gold hoop earring to one ear for the classic pirate look. You can also enhance the look with additional pirate attire like a coat or an eye patch if desired.

Elegant Sugar Skull

What You Need:

White face paint – to create a smooth, flawless base.

Black face paint or eyeliner – for creating the intricate sugar skull details.

Makeup brushes – various sizes for precise application and blending.

Setting spray – to ensure the makeup lasts throughout your event.

How to Create the Look:

Base: Start by applying a layer of white face paint evenly across your entire face. This will serve as the base for your sugar skull design, giving your skin a smooth, ghostly appearance. Make sure the paint is well blended and covers all areas evenly.

Eyes: Use black face paint or eyeshadow to create large, circular hollows around your eyes, extending up to your brows and down to your cheekbones. Blend the edges slightly for a smooth transition. Add detailed patterns around the eyes by drawing petal-like shapes to mimic the traditional sugar skull design. These can be done with black eyeliner for precision.

Nose: Paint the tip of your nose in a black triangular or inverted heart shape to mimic a skull's nasal cavity. Make sure the edges are sharp and well-defined.

Mouth: Draw thin black lines extending from the corners of your mouth outward, across the cheeks, to create a skeletal, stitched-mouth effect. Add small vertical lines along these extended lines to represent teeth. You can also draw a small line down the center of the lips to add depth to the design.

Forehead and Cheeks: Create additional sugar skull patterns on your forehead and cheeks, such as filigree, dots, or small swirls, using black face paint or eyeliner. These details should be symmetrical to maintain the elegant and traditional look of a sugar skull.

Final Touches and Setting: After completing the design, use a setting spray to lock in the makeup, ensuring it remains vibrant and intact throughout your event.

Outfit: Pair this makeup with a sleek, black suit and tie to complete the "Elegant Sugar Skull" look, perfect for a Day of the Dead celebration or any Halloween event where you want to combine tradition with sophistication.

Dark Knight Skull

What You Need:

White face paint – to create the base for the skull.

Black face paint – for creating the bold, bat-inspired and skull details.

Makeup brushes – various sizes for precise application and blending.

Setting spray – to ensure the makeup lasts throughout your event.

How to Create the Look:

Base: Start by applying a layer of white face paint evenly across your entire face. This will serve as the base for your skull design, providing a stark contrast to the dark elements that will be added later. Blend well to create a smooth and even surface.

Forehead: Begin by using black face paint to create a large bat symbol on the forehead. Extend the black paint around the symbol, covering the upper half of the forehead. Blend the edges slightly to create a smoky effect where the black meets the white base.

Eyes: Use black face paint to create large, hollowed-out areas around the eyes, mimicking the appearance of a skull. Blend the edges slightly into the white paint to give the eyes depth. Add small white dots or highlights around the eyes to enhance the skull-like appearance and add contrast.

Nose and Mouth: Paint the tip of the nose in black, shaping it into a triangular or skull-like form. For the mouth, draw thin black lines extending from the corners of the mouth towards the cheeks, creating a skeletal grin. Add sharp, bat-wing details at the corners of the mouth for a unique twist.

Chin: On the chin, create a pointed black design that mirrors the bat symbol on the forehead. Blend the edges slightly into the white paint for continuity.

Final Touches and Setting: After completing the design, use a setting spray to lock in the makeup, ensuring it remains vibrant and intact throughout your event.

Warrior King

What You Need:

Bronze or gold face paint – to create a regal, metallic base.

Dark blue face paint – for creating the bold warrior markings.

Black eyeliner or face paint – to outline and enhance details.

Gold or metallic face gem – for adding a royal accent.

Makeup brushes – various sizes for precise application and blending.

Setting spray – to ensure the makeup stays intact throughout your event.

How to Create the Look:

Base: Start by applying bronze or gold face paint to the forehead, temples, and down the sides of the face, creating a regal, metallic effect. Blend the paint well into the skin to give it a natural, yet striking, sheen. This will serve as the base for the warrior markings, symbolizing strength and royalty.

Eyes: Use dark blue face paint to create large, circular areas around the eyes. Extend the paint slightly outwards towards the temples, and downward towards the cheekbones, forming a bold mask-like effect. Ensure the shapes are symmetrical and the edges are sharp, giving the look a disciplined, warrior-like appearance.

Forehead Marking: Create a vertical arrow or spear-like design down the center of the forehead, using the dark blue face paint. Start from the hairline and extend down to the bridge of the nose. Add a small, gold or metallic face gem at the center of the design to symbolize leadership and royal authority.

Details: Use black eyeliner or face paint to outline the blue areas and add small details like lines or dots around the eyes and forehead. These details should be sharp and precise, adding to the overall warrior aesthetic.

Final Touches and Setting: After completing the design, use a setting spray to lock in the makeup, ensuring it remains vibrant and intact throughout your event.

Terrifying Clown

What You Need:

White face paint – to create the classic, ghostly clown base.

Red face paint or liquid lipstick – for the iconic, sinister smile and facial accents.

Black face paint or eyeliner – to outline and define the features.

Red clown nose – to complete the classic clown appearance.

Orange wig or temporary hair dye – to recreate the vibrant, unsettling hair.

Makeup brushes and sponges – for applying and blending the makeup.

Setting spray – to ensure the makeup lasts throughout your event.

How to Create the Look:

Base: Start by applying a thick layer of white face paint evenly across your entire face, including the neck if it will be visible. This will serve as the base, giving your skin a smooth, eerie appearance. Blend well to avoid streaks and ensure full coverage.

Eyes and Brow: Use black face paint or eyeliner to darken the area around your eyes, extending slightly outwards to create a sunken, menacing look. Emphasize the brow area with black lines to create a furrowed, angry expression. Make sure these lines are sharp and bold to enhance the character's intimidating presence.

Red Accents: Using red face paint or liquid lipstick, draw the signature red lines that extend from the corners of the mouth up toward the eyes, curving slightly as they go up. These lines should be symmetrical and crisp, giving the face an unsettling, almost alien appearance. Apply red paint to the lips, making them appear fuller and more pronounced, extending slightly beyond the natural lip line. Finally, place the red clown nose over your own nose or paint it on with the red face paint for a classic clown look.

Details: Add fine black lines around the red accents and the mouth to give the face more depth and to enhance the sinister vibe. You can also add small cracks or additional detailing around the forehead and eyes to mimic the look of cracked porcelain or aged skin.

Hair: Style your hair with an orange wig or use temporary orange hair dye to recreate the clown's wild, voluminous hairstyle. Ensure the hair is tousled and slightly chaotic for the most authentic look.

Final Touches and Setting: Once the makeup is complete, set it with a setting spray to ensure it stays intact throughout the event. This is especially important for maintaining the vibrant colors and sharp lines of the clown makeup.

Sith Lord

What You Need:

Red face paint – to create the striking base color.

Black face paint – for the intricate, dark tribal patterns.

Black eyeliner – for sharp detailing and precision work.

Small, black horns – to attach to the head for an intimidating, alien appearance.

Makeup brushes and sponges – various sizes for applying and blending the paints.

Setting spray – to ensure the makeup remains vibrant and intact throughout your event.

How to Create the Look:

Base: Begin by applying red face paint evenly across the entire face, including the neck if it's visible. This will serve as the bold, striking base that immediately captures attention. Make sure the application is smooth and even for a flawless finish.

Patterns: Using black face paint and a fine brush, carefully create the intricate tribal-like patterns across the face. These should be symmetrical and sharp, following the contours of the face to enhance the structure. Start from the forehead, moving down over the eyes and cheeks, and finish with bold lines on the chin and around the mouth. Pay special attention to creating a balance between the red and black areas to achieve a menacing, powerful look.

Eyes and Details: Use black eyeliner to sharpen the edges of the patterns and add additional fine details around the eyes and brows. The eyes should appear intense and focused, so consider adding some black eyeshadow to deepen the area around the eyes for extra drama.

Horns: Attach small black horns to the forehead and temples using skin-safe adhesive. These should be positioned symmetrically to create a balanced, yet fierce appearance. The horns are essential to completing the otherworldly, Sith Lord look.

Final Touches and Setting: After all the patterns and details are complete, use a setting spray to lock the makeup in place. This will ensure that the bold colors and intricate designs stay vibrant throughout your event.

Mystical Warrior

What You Need:

Gold and black face paint – to create the intricate, mystical designs.

Black eyeliner – for sharp detailing and precision work.

Makeup brushes – various sizes for applying and blending the paints.

Gold or metallic accents – for highlighting specific areas of the design.

Setting spray – to ensure the makeup remains vibrant and intact throughout your event.

How to Create the Look:

Base: Start by applying a layer of gold face paint to the forehead and cheekbones. This will create the base for the mystical design, giving the skin a rich, glowing appearance. Blend well to ensure the gold covers the desired areas evenly.

Eyes: Use black face paint to create large, mask-like shapes around the eyes, extending down towards the cheekbones and up towards the temples. This should resemble a warrior's mask, providing a sharp contrast to the gold base. Blend the edges slightly for a smooth transition between the colors.

Forehead Design: On the center of the forehead, use black face paint to draw an elaborate, symmetrical design that extends towards the hairline and down towards the eyebrows. Add small, precise details using black eyeliner to create intricate patterns that mimic ancient, mystical symbols. Highlight specific parts of the design with gold or metallic accents to add depth and enhance the regal appearance.

Facial Details: Continue the black paint down from the eyes, creating angular lines that define the cheekbones and jawline. Add small, detailed patterns around the mouth and chin, mimicking the look of ceremonial war paint. The key is symmetry and precision, making the design look both powerful and mysterious.

Lips and Beard: Paint the lips black and add gold or metallic highlights to the center for a striking effect. If desired, you can extend the black paint downwards from the lower lip to create a pointed beard-like design, enhancing the warrior aesthetic.

Final Touches and Setting: Once all the designs are complete, set the makeup with a setting spray to ensure it stays in place throughout your event. Double-check that all lines are sharp and the colors are vibrant, giving the final look a polished, professional finish.

Vibranium Panther

What You Need:

Black and dark purple face paint – to create the base and define the panther's powerful presence.

Silver or metallic face paint – for highlighting and adding vibranium-like details.

Black eyeliner – for sharp detailing and precision work.

Makeup brushes – various sizes for blending and detailing.

Setting spray – to ensure the makeup stays intact and vibrant throughout your event.

How to Create the Look:

Base: Begin by applying a layer of black face paint across the entire face, creating a sleek, panther-like base. Blend in dark purple face paint around the temples, cheekbones, and jawline to add dimension and depth, mimicking the reflective sheen of vibranium.

Eyes: Use black eyeliner or face paint to create sharp, angular designs around the eyes, emphasizing the fierce, predatory gaze. Extend the design outwards to create a mask-like effect that enhances the eyes and makes them the focal point of the look.

Forehead and Cheeks: With silver or metallic face paint, add intricate designs across the forehead and down the cheeks. These should mimic the look of vibranium veins or armor, blending seamlessly with the black and purple base. The designs should be symmetrical and precise, adding a technological, yet tribal, aesthetic to the overall look.

Nose and Mouth: Use black and purple face paint to define the nose and mouth, creating a more animalistic appearance. Add small, sharp silver accents around the mouth to represent teeth or claws, enhancing the fierce, warrior-like feel of the makeup.

Final Touches: Use silver or metallic paint to add fine details around the eyes, forehead, and jawline, highlighting the contours of the face and adding to the vibranium-inspired effect. Make sure these highlights are subtle yet effective, giving the face a glowing, powerful appearance.

Undead Officer

What You Need:

White face paint – to create the pale, undead base.

Dark blue and black face paint – for creating the bruised, hollowed-out effects.

Red face paint or fake blood – for adding realistic wounds.

Black eyeliner – for defining and adding fine details.

Makeup brushes and sponges – for applying and blending the paints.

Setting spray – to ensure the makeup lasts throughout your event.

How to Create the Look:

Base: Begin by applying a layer of white face paint evenly across the entire face. This will give your skin a ghostly, undead appearance, making you look like a character who has just risen from the grave. Ensure the application is smooth and consistent for a flawless finish.

Eyes: Use dark blue face paint to create large, bruised areas around the eyes. Blend the paint outward, creating a gradient effect that makes the eyes look sunken and hollow. Add some black face paint closer to the eyes to intensify the depth and create a more skeletal appearance.

Forehead Wound: To create the realistic wound on the forehead, start by using black face paint to outline the wound area. Then, apply red face paint or fake blood within the outline to simulate fresh blood and an open wound. Add some black detailing around the edges to make the wound appear deeper and more gruesome.

Details: Use black eyeliner to add fine lines and details around the eyes, mouth, and other areas to enhance the overall undead look. Draw small cracks, veins, or additional scars on the face to add to the decayed, lifeless appearance. Add a bit of black under the lips to give the mouth a more sunken, gaunt look.

Mouth: Use a combination of dark blue and black face paint around the mouth to give it a bruised, decayed look. Add some dripping black or red paint from the corners of the mouth to mimic the appearance of dried blood or decay.

Final Touches and Setting: Once you are satisfied with the look, set the makeup with a setting spray to ensure it stays intact throughout your event. This step is crucial for maintaining the undead appearance and keeping all the colors and details sharp.

Mutant Zombie Officer

What You Need:

Green and blue face paint – to create the decaying, mutant skin tone.

White face paint – for adding contrasting undead features.

Black face paint or eyeliner – for defining details and adding depth.

Red face paint or fake blood – for creating realistic, gory wounds.

Yellow face paint – to highlight the infected, decayed areas.

Makeup brushes and sponges – for applying and blending the paints.

Setting spray – to ensure the makeup lasts throughout your event.

How to Create the Look:

Base: Begin by applying green face paint to the majority of your face, focusing on the forehead, cheeks, and jawline. Blend in blue face paint around the eyes, under the cheekbones, and along the hairline to create a bruised, decaying effect. Use white face paint to accentuate certain areas like the nose and chin, creating a stark contrast between the rotting skin and the more undead, ghostly features.

Eyes: Use black face paint to deepen the eye sockets, making them appear sunken and hollow. Blend the black with the blue face paint to give the eyes a dark, eerie **look that emphasizes the undead aspect of the character.**

Wounds and Decay: To create the gory wounds on the forehead and cheek, start by outlining the areas with black face paint. Fill in these areas with a mix of red face paint or fake blood to simulate open wounds. Add some texture by layering more fake blood or using a stippling sponge to create a realistic bloodied effect. Use yellow face paint to add details around the wounds and teeth to give them an infected, decayed appearance.

Mouth: Paint the lips with a mixture of black, blue, and green to make them appear decayed and rotting. Add small black lines around the mouth to create the effect of cracked, dry skin. Enhance the decayed look by adding small, dark veins extending from the mouth outward.

Teeth and Jaw: On the cheek, create an exposed jaw effect by painting sharp, yellow teeth against the green skin. Outline the teeth with black to give them a more defined, eerie appearance, and add red paint around the area to simulate torn flesh.

Final Touches and Setting: Once you are satisfied with the look, set the makeup with a setting spray to ensure it stays in place throughout your event. This will keep the colors vibrant and the details sharp, maintaining the horrifying, undead appearance.

Zombie Cop

What You Need:

Pale blue and gray face paint – to create a dead, decaying skin tone.

Black face paint or eyeliner – for defining the hollowed-out eyes and wounds.

Red face paint or fake blood – for creating realistic, bloody wounds.

Yellow contact lenses – to give the eyes a haunting, undead appearance.

Makeup brushes and sponges – for applying and blending the paints.

Setting spray – to ensure the makeup lasts throughout your event.

How to Create the Look:

Base: Begin by applying a mixture of pale blue and gray face paint across the entire face. This will give your skin a cold, lifeless appearance, perfect for a zombie character. Blend the colors smoothly to create a decayed, undead look that covers all exposed skin.

Eyes: Use black face paint or eyeliner to create deep, sunken circles around the eyes, extending the paint outwards to emphasize the hollowed appearance. Blend some of the blue-gray base color into the black to create a seamless transition, giving the eyes a more realistic, rotting look.

Wounds and Decay: For the wounds, start by outlining the areas with black face paint. Add red face paint or fake blood inside the outlines to simulate open, bloody wounds. Use a stippling sponge or your fingers to create a textured, realistic blood effect. Around the wounds, use black and dark blue paint to create bruising and further decay.

Forehead Wound: On the forehead, create a detailed wound that appears to be stitched or stapled together. Use black face paint to draw the stitching or staples, then add red face paint or fake blood to simulate fresh blood around the wound. Highlight the edges with white or pale gray to give the wound depth.

Mouth: Paint the lips with a mix of dark purple and gray to make them look dry and lifeless. Add small black lines extending from the corners of the mouth to give the appearance of cracked, dry skin.

Final Touches and Setting: Once the makeup is complete, insert yellow contact lenses to give your eyes a haunting, undead look. Finish by setting the makeup with a setting spray to ensure it stays in place throughout your event. This will keep the colors vibrant and the details sharp, maintaining the horrifying, undead appearance.

Haunted Scarecrow

What You Need:

White face paint – to create a ghostly, pale base.

Black face paint or eyeliner – for creating the haunting details and shadows.

Purple eyeshadow – to add depth and a sinister vibe around the eyes.

Makeup brushes and sponges – for applying and blending the paints.

A scarecrow hat and accessories – to complete the look, such as straw, a burlap hat, and a rustic costume.

Setting spray – to ensure the makeup lasts throughout your event.

How to Create the Look:

Base: Begin by applying white face paint evenly across the entire face to create a pale, ghostly base. This will serve as the foundation for the haunting scarecrow appearance. Make sure the coverage is smooth and even for a flawless finish.

Eyes: Use black face paint or eyeliner to create deep, hollowed-out areas around the eyes, extending the paint slightly outward to mimic the shape of exaggerated, sinister eyes. Blend purple eyeshadow around the edges of the black to add depth and a slightly eerie undertone. This will give the eyes a haunting, otherworldly appearance.

Nose and Mouth: Paint the nose with black face paint in a triangular shape, mimicking the look of a stitched-on, rustic scarecrow nose. For the mouth, use black face paint or eyeliner to draw thin lines extending from the corners of the mouth outward, then add vertical "stitch" marks across these lines to create the classic scarecrow stitched-mouth effect.

Forehead Details: Add thin, sharp lines extending from the forehead down towards the eyes, mimicking the look of cracks or stitched seams. These should be symmetrical and sharp to enhance the overall haunted aesthetic.

Final Touches: Once the makeup is complete, put on the scarecrow hat and any other accessories like a rustic coat, a straw wig, or a burlap scarf. You can also add some fake straw to your costume to enhance the scarecrow effect.

Setting: Finish by setting the makeup with a setting spray to ensure it stays intact throughout your event. This will keep the colors vibrant and the details sharp, ensuring your haunted scarecrow look remains effective and eerie all night long.

Dark Priest

What You Need:

White face paint – to create a pale, ghostly base.

Black face paint or eyeliner – for creating the dark, hollowed eye effects and other details.

Purple eyeshadow – to add depth around the eyes.

Black lipstick – for the lips and additional detailing.

A cross or similar religious symbol – to affix to the forehead.

Makeup brushes and sponges – for precise application and blending.

Setting spray – to ensure the makeup lasts throughout your event.

How to Create the Look:

Base: Start by applying white face paint evenly across the entire face, creating a smooth, pale base that gives an ethereal, almost otherworldly appearance. Make sure the paint is evenly distributed and covers all visible skin for a flawless look.

Eyes: Use black face paint or eyeliner to create dark, hollowed-out areas around the eyes, extending slightly beyond the natural eye contours. Blend the black into a smoky effect using purple eyeshadow around the edges to add depth and a haunting, shadowy appearance.

Forehead Cross: Place a cross or a similar religious symbol on the center of the forehead. You can either affix a small, decorative cross using skin-safe adhesive or paint it on using black face paint. Ensure the symbol is centered and symmetrical for maximum impact.

Mouth: Apply black lipstick to the lips, shaping them into a sharp, defined form. Add a touch of purple around the edges of the lips to tie in with the eye makeup, giving the lips a more dimensional, dramatic look.

Details: Use black eyeliner to add fine, sharp lines extending from the eyes and lips, creating a cracked or spiderweb effect. This adds to the dark, ominous vibe of the character.

Final Touches and Accessories: Once the makeup is complete, add accessories like a rosary, a priest's collar, and black or white religious garments to complete the "Dark Priest" look. Pearl earrings or other minimalistic jewelry can also enhance the overall aesthetic.

Fallen Angel

What You Need:

White face paint – to create the pale, ethereal base.

Black face paint or eyeliner – for defining the eyes, nose, and other intricate details.

Gray or silver eyeshadow – to add depth around the eyes and accentuate the features.

Black lipstick – for the lips and additional detailing.

Small star or cross decals – to place on the forehead for a celestial touch.

Wing accessories – to complete the angelic look.

Makeup brushes and sponges – for precise application and blending.

Setting spray – to ensure the makeup stays intact throughout your event.

How to Create the Look:

Base: Start by applying a smooth layer of white face paint evenly across the entire face, creating a flawless, ghostly base that represents the purity and otherworldly nature of an angel. Make sure the paint is well blended and covers all exposed skin.

Eyes: Use black face paint or eyeliner to create deep, dramatic circles around the eyes, blending outwards for a smoky effect. Add gray or silver eyeshadow around the edges to give the eyes a shadowy, ethereal look. This will enhance the haunting, fallen aspect of the angel.

Nose and Mouth: Paint the nose in black, shaping it into a simple triangular or skull-like form. For the mouth, use black lipstick to outline the lips sharply, and then draw thin, stitch-like lines extending from the corners of the mouth outward, mimicking the look of a stitched or sewn-shut mouth. Add a small black design below the lower lip for extra detail.

Forehead and Details: Place small star or cross decals in the center of the forehead, or paint them on using black face paint. Surround these with additional fine lines or dots to create a celestial design. Add similar small designs on the cheeks or around the eyes to enhance the mystical, divine appearance.

Final Touches: Add white or silver wings to your costume to complete the "Fallen Angel" look. You can also include jewelry like silver or gothic-style earrings to add to the overall aesthetic.

Zombie Santa

What You Need:

Green face paint – to create the undead, zombie skin tone.

Purple and black face paint or eyeshadow – for creating the sunken eyes and bruised effects.

Red face paint or fake blood – for adding realistic, gory wounds.

White face paint – for highlights and enhancing the undead look.

Makeup brushes and sponges – for applying and blending the paints.

Santa hat and costume – to complete the character.

Setting spray – to ensure the makeup lasts throughout your event.

How to Create the Look:

Base: Begin by applying a layer of green face paint evenly across the entire face, giving your skin a decayed, zombie appearance. Blend in some white face paint around the high points of the face (such as the cheekbones, nose, and forehead) to add dimension and create a more lifeless, undead look.

Eyes: Use a combination of purple and black face paint or eyeshadow to create deep, sunken eye sockets. Blend these colors outwards to create a bruised effect around the eyes, giving Santa a tired and terrifying appearance. Make sure to extend the color slightly beyond the natural eye contours to enhance the zombie effect.

Wounds: To create the gory wounds, start by using red face paint or fake blood to outline the areas where you want the wounds to be. Fill in these areas with a mixture of red and black paint to simulate blood and torn flesh. For added realism, apply some fake blood using a stippling sponge to create a splatter effect around the wounds. You can also add small props like screws or bolts to the wounds for a more grotesque look.

Mouth and Beard: Paint the lips with a combination of red and green face paint to make them look decayed and infected. If you have a Santa beard, use some fake blood to add splatters or stains, making it look as if even Santa's iconic beard hasn't escaped the zombie transformation.

Final Touches: Add a Santa hat and costume to complete the look, ensuring that the hat sits slightly askew for a more disheveled, undead appearance.

Ghostly Trickster

What You Need:

White face paint – to create the ghostly, pale base.

Purple eyeshadow or face paint – for the dark, haunting eye circles.

Black face paint or eyeliner – for adding details and enhancing facial features.

Red lipstick – to create the bold, sinister lips.

Green hair spray or temporary dye – for the wild, chaotic hair.

Makeup brushes and sponges – for precise application and blending.

Setting spray – to ensure the makeup lasts throughout your event.

How to Create the Look:

Base: Start by applying a smooth layer of white face paint evenly across the entire face, creating a ghostly, almost otherworldly appearance. This will serve as the base for the trickster's eerie, clown-like look. Blend the paint evenly to ensure a flawless finish.

Eyes: Use purple eyeshadow or face paint to create dark, exaggerated circles around the eyes. Blend the edges outwards to create a smoky, haunting effect that draws attention to the eyes and gives them a deep, sunken appearance. For added intensity, you can line the eyes with black eyeliner, extending the lines slightly outward to enhance the dramatic look.

Details: Use black face paint or eyeliner to add fine lines and wrinkles across the forehead, around the eyes, and down the cheeks. These lines should be sharp and deliberate, mimicking the look of age or stress, giving the character a more menacing and chaotic vibe.

Mouth: Apply red lipstick to the lips, shaping them into a sharp, defined form that contrasts starkly with the white face paint. You can extend the corners slightly outward to create a more exaggerated, sinister smile. Add thin black lines around the mouth to create the illusion of cracks or stitches, enhancing the ghostly, trickster aesthetic.

Hair: Use green hair spray or temporary dye to color the hair, giving it a wild, chaotic look. Tousle the hair to add volume and create a more unkempt, eerie appearance. The hair should look slightly disheveled, adding to the overall crazed appearance of the character.

Final Touches: Pair the makeup with a vibrant, mismatched outfit that combines bright colors like purple and green, along with bold patterns. Consider adding a bow tie or some quirky accessories to complete the trickster look.

Demonic Fiend

What You Need:

White face paint – to create the pale, otherworldly base.

Black face paint or eyeliner – for defining the eyes, horns, and intricate details.

Red face paint – for adding a touch of sinister color to the lips and accentuating the demonic features.

Small red horns – to attach to the forehead for a devilish look.

Makeup brushes and sponges – for precise application and blending.

Setting spray – to ensure the makeup stays intact throughout your event.

How to Create the Look:

Base: Begin by applying a smooth, even layer of white face paint across your entire face. This will serve as the base, giving your skin a ghostly, demonic appearance. Ensure the paint is well-blended and covers all exposed areas of the face.

Eyes: Use black face paint or eyeliner to create deep, hollowed-out areas around the eyes. Extend the black outwards, forming sharp, winged shapes that give the eyes a more intense, menacing look. Blend the black slightly at the edges for a smoky effect, but keep the overall shape sharp and defined.

Forehead and Cheek Details: With black face paint, create intricate, sharp designs on the forehead, extending down towards the eyes and outwards onto the cheeks. These designs should resemble flames or tendrils, giving the appearance of a dark, fiery energy emanating from within. Add similar black designs around the jawline and chin for a cohesive look.

Lips: Apply red face paint or lipstick to the lips, shaping them into a sharp, defined form that adds a touch of sinister color to the face. You can also outline the lips with black to create a more dramatic contrast.

Horns: Attach small red horns to your forehead using skin-safe adhesive. Position them symmetrically for a balanced, devilish appearance. The horns are essential to completing the demonic look and should be a focal point of the makeup.

Final Touches: Add some red or black highlights to the designs on the face, enhancing the overall depth and giving the look a more dynamic, fiery appearance. Consider styling your hair to match the wild, chaotic nature of the character, or use temporary red hair dye to tie the look together.

Galactic Warrior

What You Need:

White face paint – to create the striking, alien base.

Black and red face paint – for the bold, intricate warrior markings.

Makeup brushes – various sizes for applying and detailing the paint.

Metallic accessories – like sharp ear pieces, futuristic earrings, and a spiked collar to enhance the look.

Setting spray – to ensure the makeup lasts throughout your event.

How to Create the Look:

Base: Start by applying an even layer of white face paint across the entire face. This will serve as the base, giving your skin a sharp, extraterrestrial appearance. Blend the paint smoothly for a flawless finish that contrasts strongly with the darker details.

Markings: Use black face paint to create sharp, angular designs across the forehead, down the nose, and around the eyes. These should resemble tribal or battle markings, emphasizing the character's warrior nature. Add red accents within these designs, following the contours of the black shapes, to give the look a more dynamic, fierce quality. Make sure the designs are symmetrical and sharp for maximum impact.

Details: Add small dots and lines using red and black face paint, focusing on areas like the forehead, temples, and around the eyes. These details should enhance the warrior aesthetic, giving the look a more refined, intricate appearance. Use a fine brush to create these details with precision.

Eyes: Keep the eye makeup intense and dramatic. Use black face paint or eyeshadow to create a smoky effect around the eyes, blending it into the black and red markings. This will make the eyes stand out, giving them a piercing, almost predatory look.

Lips and Chin: Paint the lips in a natural tone or slightly muted color to keep the focus on the rest of the face. Add a small black design just below the lower lip to tie in with the overall warrior theme.

Final Touches: Add the metallic accessories to complete the look. The ear pieces, earrings, and spiked collar should all contribute to the futuristic, battle-ready aesthetic. Style the hair in braids or other intricate designs to complement the warrior theme.